SPORTS IN ACTION

Golf in Action

Hannelore Sotzek

Illustrated by Bonna Rouse

Crabtree Publishing Company

www.crabtreebooks.com

Created by Bobbie Kalman

For Gabriella Romero, Karin Sotzek, and David Sotzek—my heroes

Editor-in-Chief
Bobbie Kalman

Author
Hannelore Sotzek

Managing editor
Lynda Hale

Editors
Niki Walker
Heather Levigne
John Crossingham
Amanda Bishop

Computer design
Lynda Hale

Digital prepress
Embassy Graphics

Printer
Worzalla Publishing Company

Special thanks to
Dr. Betsy Clark, Sherry Greene, and the LPGA Foundation/LPGA Girls Golf Club;
Frank Mantua and Manor Country Club, Rockville, MD; Alan Cooper and the
American Junior Golf Association; Peter Hough; George Hough

Consultant
Kathy Murphy, LPGA Master Professional and Lead Instructor for the LPGA National
Education Program Series

Photographs
Bruce Curtis: pages 9, 10, 29 (top); Brian Drake/SportsChrome: title page; Frank
Mantua/Manor Country Club: page 23 (bottom); Robert Tringali/ SportsChrome: page
31; other images by Digital Stock and Eyewire, Inc.

Illustrations
All illustrations by Bonna Rouse, except the following:
    David Calder: title page, pages 6-7, 11

Every reasonable effort has been made in obtaining authorization, where necessary, to
publish images of the athletes who appear in this book. The publishers would be
pleased to have any oversights or omissions brought
to their attention so that they may be corrected for subsequent printings.

Crabtree Publishing Company
www.crabtreebooks.com   1-800-387-7650

Cataloging in Publication Data
Sotzek, Hannelore
    Golf in action

p. cm. — (Sports in action)
Includes index.

ISBN 0-7787-0168-9- (library bound) ISBN 0-7787- 0180-8(pbk.)
This book introduces the techniques, equipment, rules, and safety requirements for golf.

1. Golf—Juvenile literature. [1. Golf.] I. Rouse, Bonna, ill. II. Title. III. Series: Kalman, Bobbie.
Sports in action.

GV968 .S68 2001

j796.352—dc21

LC 00-060391
CIP

**Published in
the United States**
PMB 16A
350 Fifth Ave.
Suite 3308
New York, NY
10118

**Published
in Canada**
616 Welland Ave.,
St. Catharines,
Ontario, Canada
L2M 5V6

**Published in the
United Kingdom**
73 Lime Walk
Headington
Oxford
0X3 7AD
United Kingdom

**Published
in Australia**
386 Mt. Alexander Rd.,
Ascot Vale (Melbourne)
V1C 3032

Contents

What is Golf?

*A player makes a stroke when he or she swings at the ball, intending to hit it. The swing is still a stroke if a player makes a **whiff**, or misses the ball.*

Golf is a quiet game that takes concentration, planning, and skill. Golfers swing specially shaped clubs to hit a small hard ball, which rests on the ground or on a peg. They aim for a small hole and try to sink the ball in it using the fewest number of **strokes**, or hits. A game, or **round**, of golf is usually made up of eighteen different holes. At the end of eighteen holes, the player with the lowest number of strokes is the winner.

Having the honor

The player who goes first has the **honor**. To start the game, the honor is determined by drawing names or by following the order on the score card. During the round, whoever gets the lowest score at a hole has the honor at the start of the next one. The player with the second lowest score shoots next, and so on. After players take their first shot, they shoot according to the distance of their ball from the hole. The person farthest from the hole shoots next.

A "wee" history

Some people believe that golf was originally played in Holland in the 1200s. In this Dutch game called *kolf,* players used a club to hit a ball at targets such as posts or doors. Many others believe the game originated in Scotland, even though there are no records of golf being played there until the 1400s. Scottish players made important developments to the game such as playing on a large area, using many types of clubs, and hitting the ball into a hole. They changed golf into the game we play today.

Welcome to the Course

Golf is played on a field called a **course**. Golf courses have nine or eighteen **holes**. Each hole is made up of a **teeing ground**, **fairway**, **hazards**, **obstacles**, **rough**, and **putting green**. The term "hole" also refers to the hole itself. The first nine holes are called the **front nine**, and the last are the **back nine**. To play a full round on a nine-hole course, players golf the holes and then play them again.

Getting from here to there

Golfers begin each hole by **teeing off**. They hit their ball from the teeing ground, which is far away from the hole. They continue to hit their ball along the fairway, one stroke at a time, until it lands on the putting green. The players then **putt**, or tap, their ball into the hole. Obstacles called **hazards** make the course more challenging.

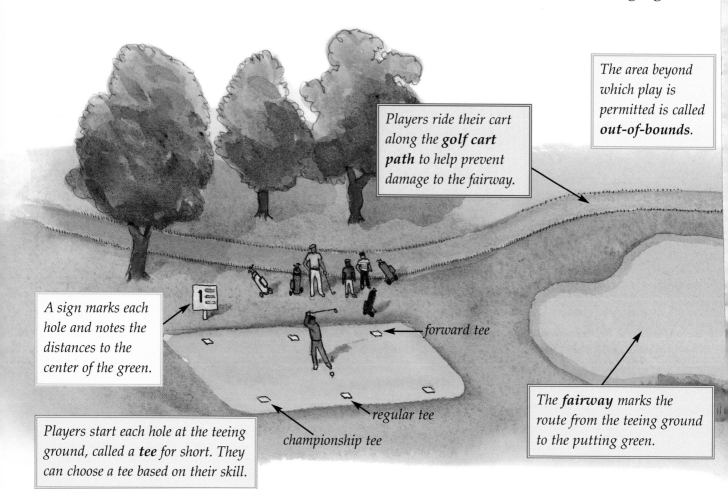

*Players ride their cart along the **golf cart path** to help prevent damage to the fairway.*

*The area beyond which play is permitted is called **out-of-bounds**.*

A sign marks each hole and notes the distances to the center of the green.

forward tee

regular tee

championship tee

*The **fairway** marks the route from the teeing ground to the putting green.*

*Players start each hole at the teeing ground, called a **tee** for short. They can choose a tee based on their skill.*

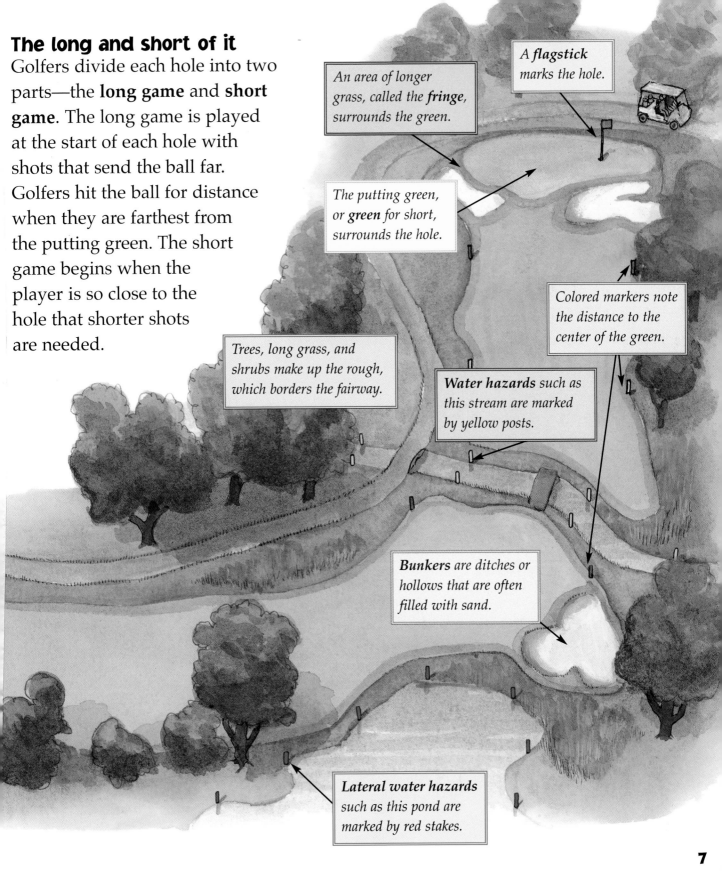

The long and short of it

Golfers divide each hole into two parts—the **long game** and **short game**. The long game is played at the start of each hole with shots that send the ball far. Golfers hit the ball for distance when they are farthest from the putting green. The short game begins when the player is so close to the hole that shorter shots are needed.

*A **flagstick** marks the hole.*

*An area of longer grass, called the **fringe**, surrounds the green.*

*The putting green, or **green** for short, surrounds the hole.*

Colored markers note the distance to the center of the green.

Trees, long grass, and shrubs make up the rough, which borders the fairway.

***Water hazards** such as this stream are marked by yellow posts.*

***Bunkers** are ditches or hollows that are often filled with sand.*

***Lateral water hazards** such as this pond are marked by red stakes.*

7

(top) The score card shows the layout of each hole on the course.

Scoring

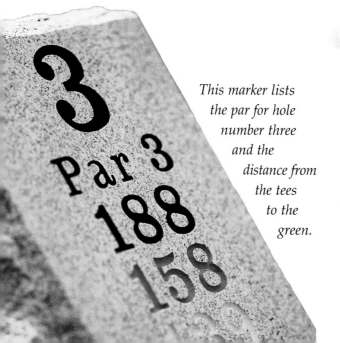

This marker lists the par for hole number three and the distance from the tees to the green.

Some holes on a course are more challenging than others. The difficulty of each hole is measured by **par**, or the number of strokes an expert player would take to sink the ball. Holes usually have a three-, four-, or five-par rating. If you add up the pars for all the holes, you get the **par for the course**. Most eighteen-hole courses have a par of 72 strokes.

An eagle is better than a birdie

Your score for each hole is compared to the par. For example, if you take four strokes on a par-three hole, you have shot one over par, or a **bogey**. A **double bogey** is two shots over par. If you sink the ball in two strokes, you are one shot under par—you score a **birdie**. Two shots under par is called an **eagle**. You get an **ace** or **hole-in-one** when you sink the ball on your first shot of each hole.

Keeping score

After you sink the ball, record the number of strokes you took on that hole. At the end of the game, add up your strokes for all the holes. During a casual game, the members of a group of golfers record their scores on the same card. During a tournament, each golfer keeps score for his or her partner. Both you and your partner must sign the card to show that the scores are correct.

Leveling the playing field

A **handicap** is a rating of how well you play based on the number of strokes you usually take. Better players have a lower handicap. Handicaps are used to adjust players' scores, allowing less-experienced golfers to compete against those with more skill. See the box on the right to get a general idea of what your handicap might be. Consult the **United States Golfing Association** or your local golf association to determine your official handicap.

*At the end of a tournament game, players hand in their cards to a **scorekeeper**. He or she records the scores, ensures they are correct, and determines the winner for the game.*

Finding your handicap

1. Play ten games of eighteen holes. Then add up your scores:
98+96+99+96+89+92+99+97+95+99 = 960
2. Divide the total by ten:
*960÷10 = 96 — this is your **average** score*
3. Now subtract the par for the course from your average score:
96-72 = 24 — this is your handicap rating
To use your handicap in a game, add up your score for a full round. For example, your score may total 99. Subtract your handicap from this total.
*99-24 = 75 — this is your **net** score*

The Essentials

Golf requires special equipment. Each golfer needs golf balls, tees, and a set of clubs, which are usually carried in a golf bag. Some players pull their bag behind them on a hand cart. Others drive around the course in a motorized golf cart.

Bright and comfy

Golfers usually wear comfortable, loose-fitting clothing that allows them to swing their clubs easily. Most golf courses have a **dress code**. Players must follow rules about which types of clothing are appropriate, such as collared shirts.

Players should wear a hat to protect their head from the sun.

Gloves help players hold onto their club. Most players wear only one glove.

Golfers wear clothing that is appropriate for the weather. They wear lightweight pieces when it is warm and put on extra layers if it is cooler.

*Golf shoes must be comfortable for walking long distances. **Cleats**, or spikes, on the soles grip the ground to give players better traction.*

The ball

Golf balls have a rubber center and a hard covering. A number distinguishes your ball from those of the other players.

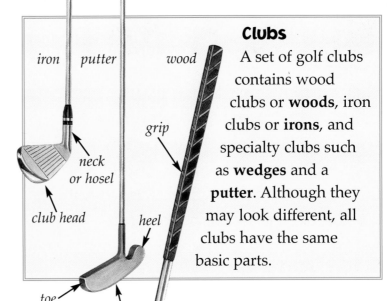

iron *putter* *wood*

grip

neck or hosel

club head *heel*

toe *sole*

shaft

Clubs

A set of golf clubs contains wood clubs or **woods**, iron clubs or **irons**, and specialty clubs such as **wedges** and a **putter**. Although they may look different, all clubs have the same basic parts.

Most wood clubs no longer have wooden heads—they are made of metal.

The shoes

Always wipe any mud from the cleats on your shoes. Replace damaged or worn cleats. Air out your shoes by loosening the laces and pulling up the tongue.

Safety first!

Give the players around you enough space to make their shots safely.

Do not hit the ball if a player is in your way.

Yell "Fore!" to warn players that a ball is coming toward them.

If there is a threat of lightning, stop playing immediately and get off the course! Never take shelter under a tree. Metal equipment makes you a target for lightning.

clubface

grooves

Club care

Use a towel or cloth to wipe off your clubs during the game. Dirt on the head can cause the ball to fly in the wrong direction. Cleaning your clubs also helps them last longer.

In case of rain, many golfers keep an umbrella in their bag.

Warming Up

Before practicing or playing, it is important to warm up and stretch your muscles. Warming up loosens your muscles so you move more easily, and it helps prevent injuries such as muscle strains and pulls. When stretching, move slowly and do not bounce. Stretch only as far as feels comfortable.

Front lunges

Keeping your upper body straight, bend your right leg in front of you and extend your left leg back. Rest your hands on your right knee for balance and count to five. Do five lunges on each leg.

Shoulder stretch

Hold up your right arm in front of you at shoulder level. Grab your right elbow with your opposite hand. Gently pull your arm toward your body. Hold this stretch for ten seconds. Now stretch the other arm.

Side bends

Stand with your arms at shoulder-height and straight out to your sides. Bend toward your right side. Stretch down with your right arm as far as it feels comfortable and reach up with your left. Slowly stand upright. Bend toward your left side. Stretch three times on each side.

neck circles

It is easy to hurt your neck so do this stretch carefully. Stand with your feet shoulder-width apart. Keep your chin tucked toward your chest, then slowly roll your head from shoulder to shoulder. Never roll your head backward!

Calf and wrist stretch

Place your palms against a wall or bar. Keep your arms at shoulder-level. Step back with your right foot and bend your left leg. Press against the wall and slowly stretch your wrist and calf muscles. Hold this position for ten seconds. Repeat with the other leg.

Torso stretch

Stand with your feet shoulder-width apart and knees slightly bent. Rest a golf club across the back of your neck and hold each end of the club. Turn your upper body slowly to the right as far as feels comfortable. Return to the middle and repeat the stretch on your left side. Stretch five times in each direction.

Arm circles

Swing your arms in large circles. Keep making the circles smaller. Stop when your arms are straight out to the side and you are making tiny circles. Change direction. Start with small circles and finish with big ones.

Know Your Clubs

To find a set of clubs that matches your body size, first get in the ready position to hit the ball (see page 19). You can tell that you are using the proper length of club if the sole sits flat on the ground. If the club is too long for your body, the toe will be raised. If it is too short, the heel of the club will lift off the ground.

Each type of golf club has a number, which refers to the **loft**, or angle of its face. The loft affects the distance and height the club will send the ball. High-numbered clubs send the ball high into the air. Clubs with lower numbers will send the ball low and far.

A lofty game

The club loft also affects how much the ball will spin. Spin helps keep the ball in the air. The greater the loft, the more the ball will spin. **Dimples**, or indentations, on the ball also cause it to spin.

*Woods such as this 1-wood, or **driver**, are used to hit the ball for distance. They also create less backspin.*

You may need to raise the ball with a tee when using clubs with less loft.

*A more lofted club also creates **backspin**, or causes the ball to spin backward. Backspin sends the ball higher in the air and helps it stop quickly when it lands.*

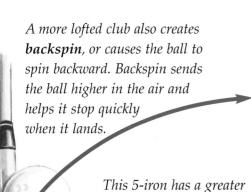

spin

This 5-iron has a greater loft than the driver. It sends the ball higher than the driver but not as far.

spin

Wedges have the greatest loft and send the ball almost straight up into the air. To create loft with other types of clubs, tilt your clubface toward the sky.

Meeting the club

When you hit the ball, strike it with the center of the clubface. The position of the club head at **impact**, or when your club meets the ball, will affect the ball's flight. The diagrams below show how to adjust the positioning of the club to direct the path of the ball in the air.

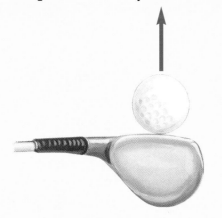

*Keep the club perpendicular to the **line of play** to hit the ball straight.*

*Rotate the club head to the left to make the ball **hook**, or curve left.*

*Rotate the club head to the right to make the ball **slice**, or curve right.*

Get the Basics

Deciding where you want to send the ball is the first step in playing golf. The next is to learn how to hold the club and position your body. Once you master these things, you will be ready for any shot!

Lining up the shot

Before you can hit the ball, you must first find your **target**, or where you want the ball to rest after you hit it. The target is at the end of your line of play, or the path you wish your ball to take when you hit it. A ball's position when it stops moving is called its **lie**. You must play the ball no matter what its lie, so landing the ball in a good spot will make your next shot easier.

Aim for a spot that is a few feet before your target. Since your ball will roll a bit when it lands, you want it to roll toward your target and not too far beyond it.

Take a stance

Your **stance** is the positioning of your feet before you take a shot. It varies according to the type of club you use and your line of play. The basic stance is the **square stance**. The **open** and **closed stances** cause the ball to curve through the air.

Feet first

Always line up your feet with your line of play. Keep your feet, knees, hips, and shoulders parallel to the line. Remember to adjust your feet only. Unless you are on the teeing ground, never move the ball with your hands!

You put your left foot in...

When making shorter shots or using shorter clubs, the ball should be in the **middle** of your stance, or between your feet. If you are using a longer club or wish to hit the ball farther or higher, keep your left foot close to the ball, or **forward** in your stance, as shown right. Sometimes you may need to shoot more to the **back** of your stance, with the ball close to your right foot, such as when hitting from a downward slope.

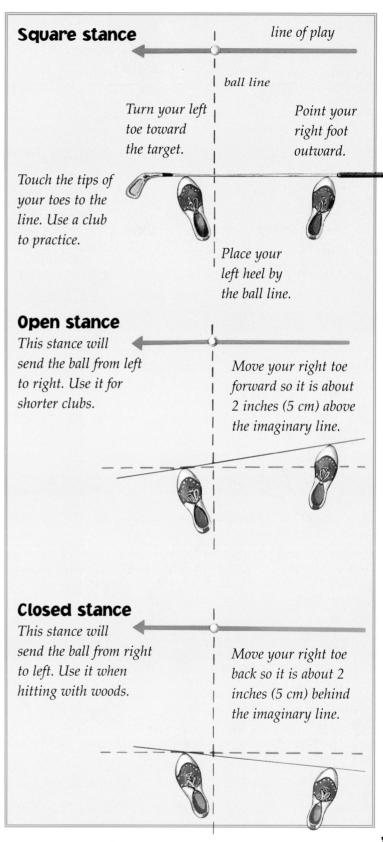

Square stance

line of play

ball line

Turn your left toe toward the target.

Point your right foot outward.

Touch the tips of your toes to the line. Use a club to practice.

Place your left heel by the ball line.

Open stance

This stance will send the ball from left to right. Use it for shorter clubs.

Move your right toe forward so it is about 2 inches (5 cm) above the imaginary line.

Closed stance

This stance will send the ball from right to left. Use it when hitting with woods.

Move your right toe back so it is about 2 inches (5 cm) behind the imaginary line.

Grips

Holding the club properly allows you to control the club as you swing and helps you send the ball in the desired direction.

Holding the club

Hold the club firmly enough to control it but not so tightly that you cannot move it easily. All the instructions in this book are written for right-handed golfers. If you are left-handed, simply reverse the instructions for left and right hands. To learn the basic hold, see the box on the right.

Hold the club at the correct angle to hit the ball properly. As you hold the club, the space between your thumb and index finger forms a "V." Imagine a straight line extending from the base of the "V" toward you. This line should point at your right shoulder.

The basic hold

Rest the club in your left hand. Extend the end about an inch (2.5 cm) past your hand. The handle should lie diagonally from the base of your palm, along the base of your fingers, and across your index finger. Wrap your fingers around the shaft and close your hand over it. Point your thumb toward the club head. Position your right hand so that the soft pad below your right thumb covers your left thumb.

Get a grip

Use one of these three **grips**, or holds, to keep your hands snugly together so that you can control your club better. Try them all to see which one works best for you. They may feel uncomfortable at first, but they should begin to feel natural with practice.

Ten-finger grip or Baseball grip
Beginners may find this grip easy to use.

Overlapping or Vardon grip
Many professional golfers use this grip.

Interlocking grip
This grip is good for players with small hands.

Putting it all together

Once you have determined your target, stance, and grip, you are ready to prepare your **address**. Your address is the position of your club and body just before you swing.

Raise your chin slightly so you are looking at the ball.

Bend at your hips and lean toward the ball. Keep your back straight.

Keep your feet, knees, hips, and shoulders parallel to your line of play.

Make sure your left arm is straight and in line with your club shaft.

Bend your knees slightly.

Place your club behind the ball, with the sole flat on the ground. The end of the club shaft should be one hand-width away from your legs.

Stand with your feet shoulder-width apart. Keep your weight evenly on your feet but not on your toes.

Place your club behind the ball. Line up the face with the target.

Perfecting Your Swing

When you swing, it is important for your hands, arms, shoulders, and lower body to work together smoothly. Remember to keep your eye on the ball through all steps of your swing!

1. Take your address.

The path your club takes when you swing is called your **swing plane**. It should **arc**, or curve through the air. Follow the same path for each step of your swing—the **backswing**, **forward swing**, and **follow through**. The pictures on these pages show a **full swing**. You can adjust this swing to suit many situations in a game. These instructions are for a right-handed player, but you can swing from the side that you are most comfortable using.

Step 1: The backswing

When you turn back with your club before you hit the ball, you make the backswing.

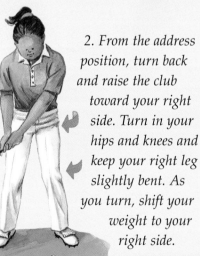

2. From the address position, turn back and raise the club toward your right side. Turn in your hips and knees and keep your right leg slightly bent. As you turn, shift your weight to your right side.

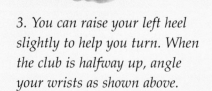

3. You can raise your left heel slightly to help you turn. When the club is halfway up, angle your wrists as shown above.

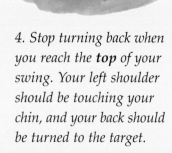

*4. Stop turning back when you reach the **top** of your swing. Your left shoulder should be touching your chin, and your back should be turned to the target.*

Step 2: The forward swing

Unwind your body during the forward swing. In this step, bring your club toward the ground and gain power to hit the ball.

1. As you swing your club down, turn your body to the left. Shift your weight from your right to left side.

2. Halfway down, start straightening your wrists and keep your left arm straight. Continue shifting your weight to help give you power.

3. As you approach the ball, your wrists should be straight. Make contact with the ball and hit it into the air.

Step 3: The follow through

*1. **Follow through**, or continue to swing, on your swing plane even after you hit the ball. Finish the arc you made during the previous steps to help ensure you hit the ball with enough force. When you are finished, your chest should face the target and you can watch the ball approach your target. All your weight should now be on your left foot. Use your right foot for support only.*

Using shorter clubs

When making shorter shots, use shorter clubs. The length of your club affects how you swing. Here are some tips on how to adjust your technique:

- Stand closer to the ball.

- Turn your body less and keep both heels on the ground during your backswing.

- Do not pull back the club too far during your backswing. Instead of bringing it behind your head, keep it vertical beside your body.

Going the Distance

At the start of each hole, you need to hit the ball a long distance to get it as close to the hole as possible. These long shots are called full swings. The full swing you make from the tee, however, is called a **drive**.

Hitting for distance

One way to make longer shots is to use longer clubs. Another way to send the ball far is to use more power when hitting it. By increasing the size of your swing plane, you can create more force to hit the ball. **Hinging**, or angling, your wrists also helps. Hinge your wrists during the backswing and straighten them on the forward swing to create more force.

You can use a tee only from the teeing ground. Insert it into the ground and rest the ball on top. Lower-numbered clubs are longer than higher-numbered ones. The longer your club, the higher you will need to insert your tee so that the center of the clubface will strike the ball.

Making a divot

When making your forward swing, you need to hit the ball solidly to send it into the air. Just before your club head reaches the ball, the **leading edge**, or bottom edge, of your club should brush along the grass. As your swing improves and you develop more power, your club will actually dig into the earth. The piece of ground you unearth is called a **divot**. Be sure to replace and pat down your divot when you finish your shot.

Practice makes perfect

You can practice all types of swings and shots at a practice area such as a **driving range**. You can work on improving how straight and far you can send the ball as well as determine which stance and grip works best for you. Practice areas also allow you to improve your balance as you swing. Good balance is necessary for an even swing.

Many practice areas also have posts to mark distances and act as targets. You can see how far you hit the ball by measuring where it lands in relation to the marker.

Remember that even the best golfer can get discouraged. If you get tired or cannot concentrate anymore, stop practicing. You are more likely to make mistakes when you not focused on what you are doing.

When practicing, be sure to allow enough room between yourself and the next golfer to avoid being hit or hurting someone else.

Shooting for the Green

Hitting a hole-in-one is rare, so you should plan to take a few shots to get your ball to the green. As you move toward the hole, there will come a point when you no longer need to make full swings. You may be so close to the green that these shots will send the ball beyond it. Bends and obstacles in the fairway may also cause you to take shorter shots rather than full swings.

Pitching and **chipping** are two types of shots that are useful in the short game. The **pitch** shot allows the ball to travel farther in the air than it rolls after it lands. A **chip** is a low, short shot that is meant to roll for a long distance after it lands.

To make a chip shot, pull the club back slightly. Use your upper body only, and keep your wrists straight.

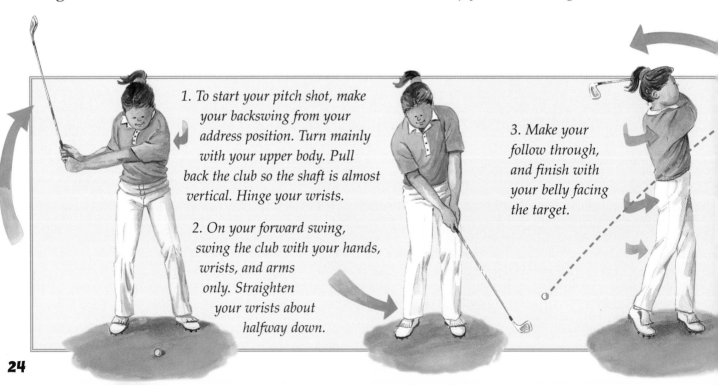

1. To start your pitch shot, make your backswing from your address position. Turn mainly with your upper body. Pull back the club so the shaft is almost vertical. Hinge your wrists.

2. On your forward swing, swing the club with your hands, wrists, and arms only. Straighten your wrists about halfway down.

3. Make your follow through, and finish with your belly facing the target.

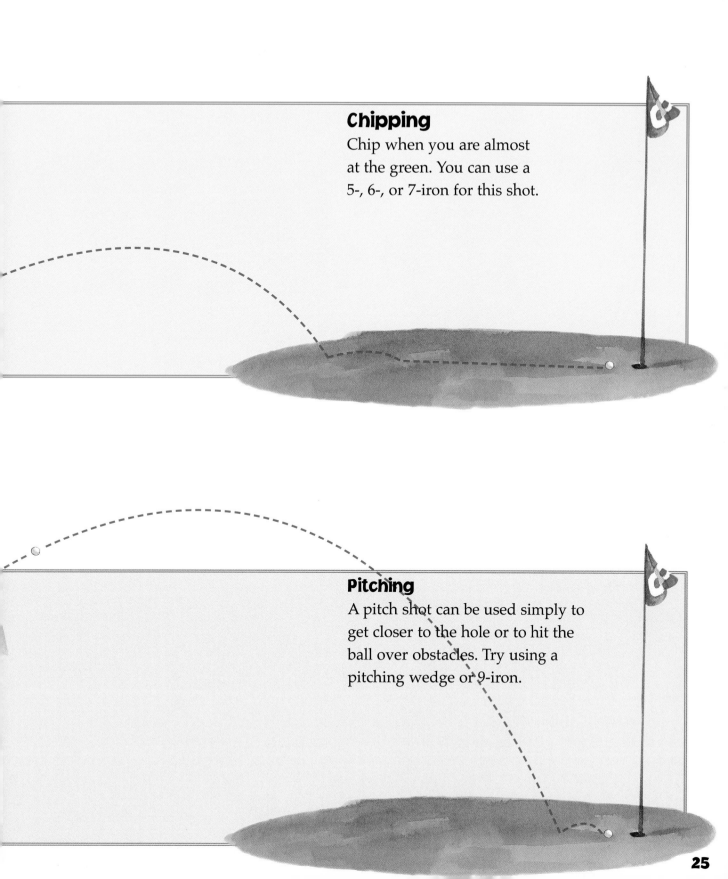

Chipping

Chip when you are almost
at the green. You can use a
5-, 6-, or 7-iron for this shot.

Pitching

A pitch shot can be used simply to
get closer to the hole or to hit the
ball over obstacles. Try using a
pitching wedge or 9-iron.

Sand Play

No matter how skilled a golfer you are, sooner or later you will have to deal with a bunker. You can waste strokes by swinging uselessly at a ball trapped in the sand. Learn to adjust your shot so that you can knock your ball clear of the bunker with just one swing.

In the bunker

Use a **splash** or **explosion** shot to escape from a bunker. With this shot, you do not actually hit the ball. Instead, your clubface hits the sand behind it to send the ball flying. Use a sand or pitching wedge for sand play.

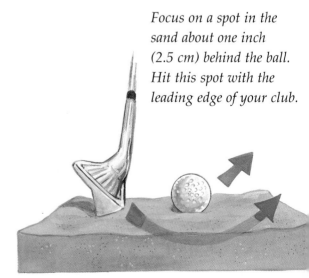

Focus on a spot in the sand about one inch (2.5 cm) behind the ball. Hit this spot with the leading edge of your club.

The Splash or Explosion Shot

Making the splash shot is like pitching —it makes the ball travel farther through the air than along the ground.

1. The ball should be forward in your stance. Keep your weight on your left foot. You can wiggle your feet into the sand for more support.

2. Keep an open clubface. Make sure that your club is not touching the sand during your address.

3. Make your backswing until the shaft is almost vertical.

4. On your downswing, the club should slide smoothly into the sand just behind the ball. Do not let the club actually touch the ball. Follow through on your swing.

5. Remember to smooth out any footprints and fill in your divot before you leave the bunker.

A buried ball

When a ball is **plugged**, or buried in the sand, you will need to adjust the splash shot. You can use a pitching wedge or 9-iron to make this shot.

1. Stand with your feet wide apart. The ball should be in the center or toward the back of your stance. Make sure the club is not resting on the sand.
2. Keep most of your weight on your left leg and make your backswing. Hinge your wrists slightly as you swing.
3. Swing down. The leading edge of the club should dig into the sand behind the ball.

On the Green

Once the ball is on the green, most golfers putt it. A putt rolls the ball along the ground instead of lifting it into the air, so putting requires a different technique than other swings. Most golfers make almost half of their strokes on the putting green. Good putting skills are the key to a low score.

Green rules

Before you can play on the green, remove the flagstick from the hole. Lay it on the grass and away from the hole. Someone can hold the flagstick over the hole to show you its location if you are making a long putt. Be careful not to hit the person or flagstick with the ball.

Putting form

1. The putter is shaped differently than other clubs. Hold it so that both palms are parallel to the shaft. Wrap your hands around it and make sure both thumbs are on top of the shaft and pointing toward the club head.
2. Aim the clubface in the direction you want to send the ball.
3. Take a square stance. Keep your feet close together but not touching. Be in the middle of your stance.
4. Pull the putter back but do not raise it. Swing with your arms only. Keep your lower body still.
5. Swing the club smoothly and hit the ball along the line of putt.

*Before you begin, determine your **line of putt**, or the path you want your ball to follow to your target. As you aim for the hole, imagine there is a large circle around it. It is okay if you hit the ball past the target when you putt—as long as you keep it in the circle so that it is close to the hole.*

Break

When putting, consider the **break** of the putt. The break is the curved path the ball takes because of conditions on the green, such as the slope. If the green slopes upward, you will have to hit the ball so it eventually rolls back toward the hole. If the green slopes downward, you should barely tap the ball—the slope will help it roll all the way to the hole.

Speed

The **speed** of the green refers to how fast the ball will roll on it. It affects how hard you must hit the ball. Hard and dry ground or very short grass creates a **fast** green. Hit the ball with less force so it will not go too far beyond the target. Wet or longer grass create a **slow** green—so hit the ball more firmly. The **grain** of the grass, or the direction in which it is growing, also affects how hard you need to hit the ball. Putting in the same direction as the grain will cause the ball to move more quickly than when you putt against it.

Miniature golf

A round of miniature golf, shown right, is a fun way to practice your putting skills. Dips, curves, and hills along the course challenge your skills and provide obstacles similar to those on a real golf course. You can make a putting area in your backyard by using buckets, bins, and plastic cups as holes.

(above) To determine how the ground slopes, squat behind the ball. Imagine which way water would flow if you poured it onto the green.

Observing the Rules

The rules of golf are determined by the United States Golfing Association, or **USGA**. During some golf tournaments, officials judge the match and enforce the rules. In a casual game of golf, however, there are no officials to watch over the golfers. Players must observe the rules themselves. They also watch fellow players to make sure that everyone plays fairly.

A **penalty stroke** is an extra stroke added to your score if you violate the rules or have to adjust the position of the ball during play. For example, you are penalized if your ball lands in a water hazard. A lost ball or one that is out-of-bounds will also cost you extra strokes. Aiding the ball by blowing it or by touching it in any way while it is moving is definitely against the rules!

It's all one big lie

Playing a ball from wherever it lies is challenging because golfers are not allowed to change the conditions around them. Players may not press down lumps in the ground, fill in hollows, or remove objects such as rocks and twigs. There are some instances, however, when you can adjust your lie. If your ball has landed in an **unplayable lie**, such as against a wall or in a tree, you may move the ball two club lengths away from where it rests. Be aware that you will be penalized for doing so. Players on the putting green may move objects as long as they do not change the surface of the green.

As long as you can swing your club safely, you must try swinging at the ball even when shrubs and long grass are in the way.

Mind your manners!

By observing proper golfing **etiquette**, or behavior, on the golf course, you will play a safer game. Most golfers would rather play with a less-skilled golfer than with someone who has poor golfing etiquette. Here are some basic etiquette guides.

- Be on time for your game.

- Make your shots without wasting the time of others.

- Be quiet when other people are making their shots.

- Let groups who are playing more quickly **play through**, or pass you on the course.

- Do not stand too close to the hole or the other players when they are making a shot.

- Leave the putting green as soon as all the players have sunk their balls.

- Make sure you leave the course in proper order. Repair any divots on the teeing ground, fairway, and bunkers. Repair any damage you made to the green with your ball or the spikes on your shoes. Rake any footprints made in the sand.

Golf Words

address A player's position when he or she has taken a stance and placed the club in a position to hit the ball

chip shot A low, short shot that rolls far on landing

drive A full swing made from the tee

hazard An obstacle on the course, which can only be a bunker, water hazard, or lateral water hazard

hole (1) A numbered section of a course; (2) The hole into which players sink their ball to finish each section

honor The player who shoots first from the tee

lateral water hazard A water hazard over which a player does not have to hit the ball in order to reach the hole

lie The position of the ball when it is at rest

line of play The intended direction of the ball after it has been hit along the course

line of putt The intended direction of the ball when it has been hit on the putting green

net score A player's final score in a game

par The difficulty level of a hole; or, the number of strokes it would take an expert player to sink the ball

pitch shot A high shot that rolls a little on landing

putt A shot made by tapping the ball so that it rolls only along the ground

splash shot A shot made to escape from a bunker; also called an explosion shot

stance The placement of a player's feet when he or she is ready to take a shot

stroke A forward swing of the club made with the intention of hitting the ball

tee (1) The teeing ground; (2) A small peg on which the ball rests at the start of a hole

unplayable lie Describing the positioning of the ball that is impossible for a player to play

water hazard A hazard filled with water over which a player must send his or her ball in order to reach the hole

Index

3 4 5 6 7 8 9 0   Printed in the U.S.A.   9 8 7 6 5